EVENT HORIZON

ALSO BY CATE MARVIN

Oracle

Fragment of the Head of a Queen

Legitimate Dangers: American Poets of the New Century,
edited with Michael Dumanis

World's Tallest Disaster

EVENT HORIZON
CATE MARVIN

Copper Canyon Press
Port Townsend, Washington

Cover art by Marina Font: (front) *Personal Space,* 2017. Archival pigment print on cotton rag paper, gesso, and thread, 17 × 13 inches; (back) *Red Drops,* 2017. Archival pigment print on cotton rag paper, gesso, and thread, 13 × 9 inches.

Copper Canyon Press is in residence at Fort Worden State Park in Port Townsend, Washington, under the auspices of Centrum. Centrum is a gathering place for artists and creative thinkers from around the world, students of all ages and backgrounds, and audiences seeking extraordinary cultural enrichment.

LIBRARY OF CONGRESS CATALOGING-IN-PUBLICATION DATA

Names: Marvin, Cate, 1969– author.
Title: Event horizon / Cate Marvin.
Description: Port Townsend, Washington : Copper Canyon Press, 2022. |
    Summary: "A collection of poems by Cate Marvin"— Provided by publisher.
Identifiers: LCCN 2021053278 (print) | LCCN 2021053279 (ebook) |
ISBN 9781556596438 (paperback) | ISBN 9781619322554 (epub)
Subjects: LCGFT: Poetry.
Classification: LCC PS3563.A74294 E94 2022 (print) | LCC PS3563.A74294
    (ebook) | DDC 811/.54—dc23/eng/20211029
LC record available at https://lccn.loc.gov/2021053278
LC ebook record available at https://lccn.loc.gov/2021053279

9 8 7 6 5 4 3 2 FIRST PRINTING

COPPER CANYON PRESS

Post Office Box 271
Port Townsend, Washington 98368
www.coppercanyonpress.org

for Emerson

I know the Wire-Puller intimately
And if it were not for the people
On whom you keep one eye
You could look straight at me
And Time would be set back

Mina Loy

CONTENTS

EVENT HORIZON

Lottery of Eyes

My daughter learns how to read with eyes
I can't claim to know the color of
though they started out gray then turned
green, and were one day blue,
and naysayers who said they'd turn brown
were wrong, they are like leaves
to be sure, but they are mostly like the colors

that move windward over the surfaces of lakes,
little scuffles or scallops or shells
of tiny waves combed across a brilliant surface:
I cannot answer yes or no when my
daughter asks if her eyes are green. Can you not
look inside your own eyes to find
what color they are? Too bad our eyes cannot

speak the colors they feel, be changing things,
the shade of iris accompanying
the brow in temperament. When my daughter
first learned to drop into a book,
she left, she turned off by turning on, her face
canceling all reward: recalling
to me the time she was points only, three dots

on the printout of the sonogram, below which
someone assigned the word TOES
because she'd already learned to disappear. When
she first appeared, she was not
unlike a slice of paper that's gotten lost inside
the photocopier, frustrating
the machine, getting shredded in its making.

Who are you and how? I just lost this document,
which was an entire poem,
which was not unlike my daughter's twin who
would know by now how to read
if she did not run red down my inner leg while
I was reading. How was it that
I was able in the first place to give birth to a pair

of eyes? Giving birth is the opposite of being
swallowed. Trying to make that
match catch, kindle a being, it's as impossible
as scooping the eye's net through
a fish tank stocked with the alphabet: who can
know what and who you will be
lucky enough to catch? One fell out the bubblegum

machine of my uterus, a blood rush sucked into
the godless mouth of the toilet,
but this one is sitting across from me right now,
reading a book, and even tonight
she is still taken up with the question of eyes:
are hers gray or green? Typically
I'd dismiss this exchange as an exercise in vanity,

because what a miracle it is, the things eyes do!
I made this pair inside me.
I can't say exactly what color they are, but they
started out gray, then everyone
said they'd turn brown soon as a moon passed
over a cloud, but then they held
the green mirror of a leaf before them and one

day they were blue, but mostly they're lichen gray.
And what eyes might have shone

from her twin's head? The same set of moon-
hazed gray that peers from my
girl's head, or another pair of nearsighted baubles
set behind lenses like her sister's?
Love is a pair of stares that smarts like a wound!

Ice Cream in February

Sitting in this car like a worn-out century,
an ashtray on wheels—my fingers direct

its wheels to pull into this lot as tears creep
from their ends to lacquer the steering wheel.

I've positioned myself to face this faded
storefront without the foresight to see it

is what was formerly the Babies "R" Us that
swung its doors open before my feet

when all I bought was diapers and my arms
hauled plastic bags freighted with formula

and pacifiers, the cruel weight of the car
seat that hung from the crook of my arm

held suspended the jewel that was my
daughter whose cries were like ribbons

at midnight. Back then, I was always in
the market for pacifiers, diapers, and baby

formula. I'd buy cloth bibs by the dozens
because, just like I got smart about breast

milk, I got smart about all the spitting up:
if I just kept a bib on the kid and swapped

it out each time the formula dribbled up
out the baby mouth, I wouldn't have to

change the whole outfit. Baby hacks,
I guess you could call them. Mother's Day,

I happened to be in there because I was
always in there, stocking up on disposable

diapers, diaper creams, teething rings
molded out of plastic from a factory in

China, and while checking out the nice
young man I saw practically on a daily

basis said, "Happy Mother's Day, I hope
your husband got you something nice."

And in the way I had back then, one eye
always asquint, circles practically drawn

with markers beneath my eyes, hands
trembling not because I had to climb fifty

steps to my apartment with the fifty-
pound car seat encasing the fifteen-pound

baby, but because I only got to sleep in
2½ hour increments and was therefore

actually insane and even hallucinating,
I said, "My Mother's Day present to myself

is that I'm not married." Now Babies "R" Us
is shuttered forever. Now I dip the plastic

spoon into the frost, eat a barrel's worth
of sugar, which will reach down to my blood

as a stranger offers his hand to an old lady
to help her off the bench at the bus stop.

My daughter orders a pumpkin spice
latte at the drive-thru. I am alone again

in this world. For years, she spared me
from my own self-interest, got me used

to bending down for the bedtime kiss,
to waiting while she learned to manage

shower faucets, on hand to rescue her
from water's scald. Now she disappears

into steam, shutting the door behind
her. I, too, dissolve. The drive-by sky

in this nowhere lot is worse than a fat
policeman fattening himself on baked

goods inside the heated cubicle of his
vehicle's interior, as I watch him while

I eat an ice cream cone in winter, tears
leaking from the ends of my fingers, my

one lost mitten somewhere on some
road behind me, a three-lane boulevard

along which buses constantly drag
their plumes of exhaust and stores

heave a sigh and roll over onto their
sides to die their brick-and-mortar

deaths before the president of a land
in which I never requested citizenship

and the dying woman under a blanket
at the ferry station curls up inside my

ear murmuring that she forgives me
for the morning I almost dropped

a dollar into her cup but stopped when
I only found a twenty in my wallet and

did not have the time or compassion
to break it at the coffee shop because

I did not have time.   The best part
of being alone is being alone, is being

able to enjoy an ice cream cone, but now
I'm starting to sound like someone who

thrives on simple pleasures, which
just isn't true. I've always despised

those women who think trespass is
sneaking an extra chocolate, or hoarding

a favorite cookie. Come on, bitches, let's
fall down some stairs!   No one calls

me to see how my day at work is going,
and I'm always hauling the trash cans

out to the end of the drive, and at this
point in my life I just look like an old

woman to people who drive by, which
is better I guess than being harassed,

but why can't you get something in
between a leer and a disgusted smirk

for having a body that carries you to
the mailbox to find out there is no mail?

Rendezvous with Ghost

Did it transpire to rise from beneath the floorboards?
Did it escape into the room through a heating vent?
Suddenly, my head, palpable as an apple, felt its eyes.
The folding chairs woven into the room by their rows.
The shining caps of knees bent that belonged to bodies
that sat with ears attentive as rabbits struck midfield
by a passing motor. The poem being read gave us back
the image of those metallic blankets underneath which
migrant children in pictures slept. It was then I felt it.
It was not like saying *It has been so long, where have
you been,* though I felt that. It was not like saying, *Nice
you finally turned up, where's my ice cream?* And though
it did tickle, I once read about a person who was tickled
to death. It felt like the opposite of death, which means
I felt my hands lying like quiet historians on my lap,
as if my books had been alphabetized behind my back.
I'd been waiting so long I'd given up. I'd always hoped
it'd be grandiflorous, sweet as a clove cigarette, or shot
through with delinquency, circumspect. It was a fancy
fashioned from the idiocy of loneliness, bad as a shark
movie, sad as an orphan's eyes in propaganda in which
the child you sponsored did not exist. It is memory like
this. Once, we curled inside an elegy like a worm inside
a jumping bean. Afterward, I stood and left, walked
the halls of the historic hotel, found my face in a mirror,
and told no one. *But I love him. I love him. I love him.*

Nostalgia Is A

ghost just now walking into my room
wearing real clothes. Before the knock,
the truck slides softly onto its side in
snow. I was waiting for his knock. My

body falls against his body as all bodies
fall. All this long while, my ear pressed
to the door. Truck stuck fast in snow,
we pull our warm bodies out into ice air.

Ghosts require hosts, as does memory,
as does that slide grateful to gravity
of a body fallen softly on top of a body
toppled sideways in a truck so gently

swerved into a snowbank. Snow is all.
Blank and cold: mutual accounts froze.
Snow is always what we were not, no?
A ghost is no one we know if we decide

to ignore it. I am waking up. When we
give it our eyes, it takes on our bodies.
A ghost walks out, leaves its chill behind.
When I finally wake up, the first thing

I see, naturally, is light. Against fabric's
weave of floor-length curtains shot
through with filament, light sears raw
mouths open, beams amber bluffs.

Say that no matter how my steps stagger
their blood ways along this page, as my
hand, unused to script, aches along, he's
not one of any of those moons I forgot

because *because*'s a weak word, because
on that night there was no accident, yes,
we could say, of the stars, the stars who
themselves contrived to know us better

than we ever knew ourselves. Accidents
are an idea. Interrogate the scene, you'll
find there's no such thing. Yet, now falling
softly on our faces, this snow's supreme.

Two Views of a Discarded Mattress

1

Propped against a tree on a sidewalk next
to the trash cans, shorn of sheets, its fabric
a casing for its coils, harborer of secretions
seeped and dried, its phosphorous surface
glitters abandoned skin flakes in moonlight,
shingles from roofsides of humans. Mucous
trails pearlescent from a snail crawled up
the trunk of the tree upon which this bed,
formerly slept on, now leans. Loved upon?
Perhaps. Dreamt on most definitely. Hands
on skin most definitely, the stains it harbors
are the trails of dreams, the shotguns aimed
at baby carriages, molars boring holes into
the palm upon which they are cast like dice,
and the mystery of love as scratchy and fine
smelling as the needle tree that carried you
off with its scent of resin: it's a hideous thing.

2

Sheet marks on the face won't disappear into
the water filling the basin. Under the eyes dark
lakes before the resinous reflection of window
cast into mirror by interior lights set against
the night. Do you wonder if I dream of your
shattering? Marks on the face don't melt into
the water. It would be strange to dream that
hard for a stranger, even for you who became
strange within an hour. Yet I am waking from
the press of your face against my face. Carried

off over the shoulder, hauled through doorways,
receiving your murder, once this mattress was
bent at its middle, sagged profuse as a gaping
blouse, and bore stains of which I was never
aware while asleep. You knew. You were there
too. You will dream of congress between us.
I withdraw my hand. I refuse. Haul me away.

Breaking a Face

My face is a jar of honey
you can look through
Mary Ruefle

A tiny dog clothed in a fleece jacket, eyes bulging, is strung
to a man in a park where I've brought my own dog for sun.

The man takes umbrage I curse aloud when Charlie twists
his leash and my wrist, muttering it *must be your female*

nature, and the blood in my mouth is hinged on the crisp
edge of a cliff. Charlie is also the name of my father, who

hated dogs and, by that rationale, hated Charlie, who also
prefers humans to dogs, pressing always past his canine

counterparts to achieve communion with their owners,
because jealousy is not just human. And because the sun

breaks itself today at the edge of the water, dribbling bits
of itself into the gray, I cannot disallow myself to unspool

my obscenity. The man begins to back away, pulls his dog's
leash taut. Charlie pulls me: four of us stand at either ends

of leashes. Now the man backs himself across the street,
crabwise, and a glitter rises from up from the bottoms

of his eyes, twitching with his twitching dog, *Must be that*
time of the—and Charlie, a large dog, is either oblivious

to my peril or chooses not to present himself as imminent
threat, tugs my body toward a crusty snowbank, the next

chapter in the day's book of smells, pulling my arm's length
into taffy. But I wait. I want to see if this man will break

my face, to see if he will choose to break it or see that when
he breaks it, I am not my face. I do not break, though I will

perform the bleed he wants me to know he's seen. To curse
me by informing me of my own curse? Make me obscene

when he is the obscene tourist of my form? There is nothing
to do but spill fumes and oily residue, pour junk from my lips,

an embarrassment of overture, insist, as unwelcome provider
of the fantasy he wishes to deny yet to which he clings, that

the phantasmagoria of rust between the legs exists, like so
much grief. *Yeah,* I say, *the blood's spilling out my cooze,* my

free arm waving at the road, *it's pooling alongside the curbs,*
I'm washing my hands in its puddles, I'm spreading through

these streets like a disease. Then Charlie pulls me away, we
go his way, away from the man and his tiny dog in directions

I will allow him to take me, away and toward other animals
and their humans. My father didn't just hate dogs, he hated

animals in general. He wasn't a fan of children, either. When
I see red, I think of him. The first time I saw red was when

I talked to him. I was the unluckiest number. Or maybe I am,
as he would have no doubt said, *reading too much into things.*

Trying Too Hard

Back when you'd spin my friends like a record player, I wore my role
of confidant like a fur coat. Slice a finger while opening a beer can,

fizz the gin high in tumblers, I'd cling to the edge of my raft, dangle
my gashed leg into your salt water, a phosphorescence of jazz I can

still feel licking my blood. I can't remember how long I stood aglow
in your midnight kitchen with my heart pinned to that picture I can

still see stuck to the refrigerator: your best friend. Always your chum,
we were done, pressing our mouths at the edge of lover, playing "Can't

We Be Friends" over and over. Crack open an oyster and see its spit's
a pearl in a pair of earrings my grandmother couldn't afford. How can

I expect you to relate? Your grandfather owned a department store.
Did you ever love me? Fingers that wish to tremble above digits can-

not dial, compliments of that second self who erased your number.
I'm the Staten Island to your Manhattan, your Brooklyn, you can't

cross a bridge to visit me, even though the ferry is free. You don't
take mass transit, naturally. You'll be staying in Tribeca, why can't

I just meet you at the Odeon later, you're paying. Plates of oysters
I'll return to the water in the ladies' room, it's the richness I can't

keep down. Words like "unfortunately" encroach on this poem, sharks
smelling blood in water. I poured myself out like a beer can: it began

with my love for your best friend, years before you turned beautiful
again. But there was a picture of me on your fridge too. Now I can

see that *I* was your best friend. I want to call you to let you know
I just read that the Odeon has closed, forever, due to COVID. Can

I ever admit my feelings became a phantasmagoria you couldn't
handle? I am far too delicate. I've erased your number and can't.

You May Eat

I'm leaving the set of vintage flatware in my shopping cart
in the event no one else seizes it, so should I come by a windfall
I'll be able to swoop back in, purchase it, and complete myself.

We always had perfectly matching flatware in the house
in which I grew. To introduce an errant fork even, I think,
would have been blasphemous. In fact, I don't think I could

have birthed this idea myself. I only happened upon this idea
by happenstance, later in life, because of a drawer of cutlery
from out which I fish flatware, sets merged and married

between two disparate households: faced with five family
members, practicality forces one to give up coordinating.
My father always sat at the head of the table, my mother

and I at his either side, and though he had not cooked, nor
had he ever, being incapable, he'd proceed to evaluate
the meal as if he were some kind of expert chef. Once we'd

placed our napkins on our laps, we'd wait for him to allow
us to help ourselves to a serving. Wait, I'm remembering it
wrong. We never served ourselves. He served us. And once

he'd doled our portions out, he'd draw himself up and say
in mock solemnity, *You may eat.* And so in this way I nightly
became accustomed to allowance and instruction. He winced

at my voice. His foot twitched at the ankle, tapping the floor
in involuntary exasperation. The set I want most isn't that
fancy. It's the plainness I covet, that midcentury look that

would have never jived with any of my parents' furniture: the Victorian sideboard, the sleek table where we ate every night by candlelight. I'd also prefer a minimalist headstone.

The Eyes of the Neighborhood

I

The man whose girlfriend I saw moving small with the heavy
laundry basket from the Laundromat to pile herself and her

little dog into his junky car, the man whose girlfriend posted
a picture of herself with bruised wrists and eyes asking that

we fund her given she could no longer earn a living cleaning
the summer people's houses, the man whose girlfriend died

from an overdose just after she took out a restraining order
against him is sitting behind me at the market deli, still alive,

and no one is doing anything about it. He talks into his phone,
he is unencumbered, at ease, casually jabbing his fork at his

pasta salad, this man whom I've been introduced to three times
but who pretends he does not see me now that I have sat down

near him. Is no one amazed? He is at liberty. But how can it be
that the screams have been washed from the air, my goodness.

II

The screams grew out the windows like flowers mad to rise
up from the ground, the wretched ballerina with her twisted

mouth. Rampant, out her house she is flexing her body down
this street, the jugulars pumping in her neck like live ropes.

She smashes her face into the air, now stares down her target
at the dock where people sluggish wait for a ferry to depart,

and a jetsam of pending lawsuits laces the air intricate as if
etched with the tip of a small knife by a skilled hand. Crowds

coagulate by the humming metal case of the soda machine,
the bicycle rack, the wooden benches baking in the sun. Just

beyond, the water clamors with excitement, rushing its froth
from between the propeller blades like blood squeezed from

a closed fist, this is her language, not the language of pirouettes
but threat: *so shut up and take the grim future in your mouth.*

III

This child playing in a ditch beneath this afternoon sun has no
teeth, is all gums. They fed him so much sugar the roots sucked

the calcium back, withdrew their potent future, turned entirely
black. Language is coming hard for his brother, who visits, who

mostly nods, and eats what we give him with his hands. Mother
sulks, smokes, seemingly scowls from three doors down, but I

do not wear my glasses anymore as they are a hindrance against
believing this world might be interrupted any minute now by

a commercial for laundry detergent. It is a well-known fact that
when you see a certain truck turn onto the street you're walking

down, the driver is drunk, will step out while the engine idles
to stoop and piss roadside in tall grasses in daylight outside

the ballerina's house, the meth head's shack, the famous author's
porch. The sea chews its swimmers like tobacco, the stained sun.

IV

That game you played when taking the train, fixing your eyes
on the shoddiest house to conjure some other more impossible

existence. Or that palpable loneliness that had your eyes reach
for other eyes from out your car into another person's car: that

shack is what you are looking at now as you sit on the peeling
picnic bench in the backyard of the man you've tied your mouth

into a bow for. There must be a way to clean it up, plant some
flowers, impose derelict chic, boho fuckaroo, scrub the fuck out

of the floors, so you scrub until the floors give way, and it's like
getting to know someone better and better, their eyes change,

were once green, are now green but not the same, and years later
you'll hear that floor you scrubbed with no success was torn up,

all that house's floors plain rotten. But it was fun in that seaside
town, sticking ditch lilies in a vase on the kitchen table, wasn't it.

V

Arranging those ditch lilies in a vase you've placed on a table you
wouldn't bother donating to Goodwill, you're all loved up now,

aren't you? Scrubbing the floor until it disappears beneath your
actual hands, scrubbing the stain out to which you can claim no

association—honest! How'd you get here, and why won't this spot
disappear? You've tried all the cleaning solutions. You find him

on Instagram, the greasy pictures he last left on Facebook. You
see he has once again begun, his presence reassembling itself,

his knowledge slow and certain as blood seeping into a carpet.
Recall the wreath of prints around your neck, his pomegranate-

stain necklace. You are yet another woman who thought she had
to protect her husband more than herself. And like the batshit

ballerina, you too lived beneath a roof upon which moss accrued
almost kindly, with a man for whom you tied your lips into a bow.

Faces

I'm just like the rest of you, a run-out pen. Or like you
with the paper-bag hat, waiting outside the library

to get in. It's about to open, we stand facing the glass
doors at three minutes to 10:00. I can barely stand it.

Like a tree, I'm dying from the inside, shooting leaves
toward the light and making out like I'll be around

for a long time to come. Only now my heaviest branch
drops, splintering its huge, damp shard on the drive,

causing everyone to sigh their gladness that no one
was standing on that very spot, as if anyone would

ever happen to be standing beneath me, waiting for
me to do something. It's my doing nothing you come

to trust. But mine is an acrimonious relationship with
time. It feels like a wool sweater, or like the damp

squeezed out of a sweater, or like a sweater, period.
Clamped in the damp, ministering the body through

doorways, shielding the points of elbows from knives
of furniture corners. This is a dangerous world. Even

though I keep spooling out the gradual yo-yo of my
shadow along the walk with the tenderness a snail

evokes as it peers gently out its shell, you know it
could freeze at any minute, all the ice that drips from

my eyes to the concrete, tears striking countenances
like shards hit glass doors, like hail, like exclamation

points from the sky or eyes: I see you! Coming around
that corner, smile like a knife, ready to steal my life.

The Teacher Says Poems about Dreams Are Boring

for Richard Howard

But I dream about my teacher. We're reading Tennyson
who falls out from his train car in ecstasy to see the sand
that is the sea. Were we not aware that he could not see?
That this fact blurs the quality of his images, which is his

particular beauty? We drop down into the Kraken then.
It gets to me. Everyone is writing down everything. I never
used to take notes but now can't stop writing everything
he says down. My cheek's pressed so hard now against

my pillowcase my face will surely wear these lines once
it wakes. But in sleep you feel no shame. Richard could
take you into Tennyson and make you feel a man carving
his mother up in a bathtub was okay. In this dream, a man

is carving a Mother Mary scrimshaw into his mother's
thigh. It makes perfect sense to me, his need. I'm wanting
him to go harder at her. I'm not worried he's hurting her.
Richard Howard is still alive. I'm lying in bed next to one

of my husbands. By this point, I have had many husbands.
I hear that nowadays Richard can't remember anything.
A friend on the phone after we lost Adam used the word
aphasia. Richard says, *High school is, as everyone knows,*

a waste of time. I never got the lotos-eaters until I realized
I went to high school with them. Now I feel sick thinking
about them. I block them on my social media. I want to live
past 50. I'm only 24. As usual, I'm drinking too much. My

boyfriend at the time lands in jail. I don't have the cash or
know-how to bail him out. His crime is he didn't pay a bunch
of parking tickets. He calls and calls. My face acquires a tic.
I'm taking notes across from Richard at that seminar table

in 1994. We write down everything he says. We cannot get
over the luxurious Rossettis. Now he's taking us deep into
Tennyson's *In Memoriam*. Richard says, *But, my dear, you
are of course aware that*　　　　　*?* We are not. He knows

so much more than any of us. The rumor is Richard learned
the entire French language in the backseat of a car on a road
trip from Ohio to Florida as a kid. Richard is now furious with
me. I've accidentally messed up the order of photocopies he's

passed around, and his eyes stab me from behind their round
frames. *Maybe someday you should go to the library.* Now all
our eyes drop to floor and hands. I'm so angry I almost walk
out. Then I apologize. During class break a classmate says it

happens to everybody. *Kiss the ring*, another friend says. I am
terrified of Richard. Should I go back to class? *You have to kiss
the ring*, the friend insists. Years later I'm sitting in Richard's
apartment in New York. He says he has not heard from my ex-

husband, the fish, in years. Who adored Richard. This husband
owes much of his career to Richard. Who is hurt. It seems odd
to me, disgraceful even, he has neglected Richard. All the while
he's been persistent as a roach in my dreams, appearing nightly

in the kitchen of my mind, fluorescent in the audacity of his pain.
Last night he lay on my bed with his shirt unbuttoned while we
chatted about which rivers are the hardest to swim up. What
scales feel like when they loosen. He's wearing the expensive

watch I gave him. I slop on the bed, roll in moistened sheets.
Getting older, the skin gets hot and wet, spills out its regrets
from a bank account of sweat. Back then, I worried all the time
I wasn't smart enough. Back then, I was worried I didn't have

a husband yet. Which bores Richard, making it hard to explain
how my ex would do this thing where he'd jut his chin at me
in emphasis, causing this barely discernible tic beneath my left
eye. Richard shrugs. I wake up to pee. The last time I ran into

Richard, at KGB, he shrank from me as if I moved with a disease.
Did he not recognize me? I wanted to press my flesh beyond
its reserve, embrace him, but I was still afraid of him. It's 1994
again. I'm 24. *You have improved,* Adam Zagajewski says, after

months of our meeting weekly over coffee in the bookstore café.
He has seen all the poems. He says it like a coroner examining
a corpse to identify the cause of death. My writing is still very bad.
I'm sitting on Richard's red couch while he reads my poems. His

dog, a pug named Maude, licks my hand. He asks what Cynthia
said in workshop. *She didn't like them.* He says, *Well, I think they're
quite good.* And just like that he says he's going to publish one
in the *Western Humanities Review.* Decades later, explaining to

a student how to better describe the plunder of panties from
a dresser drawer in his poem, I feel Richard's stare land like
a beam on my shoulder. He stands in the doorway. I am 49.
I kiss his ring. I kiss it hard. Now he cannot not recognize me.

My Father's Daughter

It was lonely like that, sitting there, ugly like.
Sat down sudden on the stoop and lit a cigarette.
She wore a beard of smoke. She heaved with evidence.

The surveillance van hauling bones of Cold War
enemies twisted round the corner of Moody onto
Morning, its wires within conducting an analysis

of the outrageous slowing of her pulse, marking
now her departure from sense into the freeze.
The neighbor's curtains twitched with evidence.

A middle-aged lady with her head in her lap.
Across the street, curtains twitched with neighbors.
Who does that? She once cried on the subway.

This was way worse. A young woman was pushing
her baby down the same street, past the stoop
upon which her bent legs were bent, her head

dropping its deadweight against the soft denim
sheathing her knees. Dogs moved jubilant, autumn
thralled, pleased to be alongside so many legs.

Head set heavy as a metal plate atop her bent
knees, she sensed the plastic flowers stuck in
window boxes across the street were menacing

the gods. All the world was bent on a limb, was
elbowing in with its analyst crouch, hinting at its
covert codes, tapes pregnant to unspool sobs she

could spill down the step of her stoop, leak onto
the streets. How she'd liquefy dogs' happy howls
as they lapped the greasy pools of her discontent!

She sits now on a stoop atop bones like shards,
her flabby ass, as his laugh comes back up her
throat, thinking back to a dinner party when she

was ten, his one friend from work chortling as
he poured his face into a glass, *The poison gas,
my favorite project!* She looks like anybody.

Event Horizon

Remember when you stabbed me on my birthday?
A glass of wine itched, scratched itself off the table.

Whatever phones were then, they were dead.
Whatever phones were then, we can barely recall.

But numbers remain numbers and yours dialed
went unanswered. You were dead on the other end.

And no one knows about the flowers you sent, nor
the manner in which I sat through dullest hours

on my couch aiming a kitchen knife at my wrist.
That I do not choose the role of victim remains

unsaid. I sit across a table from you at a thesis
defense and by my silence advance the thesis

that I never sucked your dick like the broken stem
of a honeysuckle flower. For many years we continue

to act like I have never sucked your dick like the broken
stem of a honeysuckle flower. You'll ask if I'm willing

to recommend to my editor a manuscript you have
had trouble publishing. I'll oblige because it seems

I do not know what I am about. I adopt more cats.
I develop an exercise routine. I note you do not own

any pets. I don't get that and don't have much sympathy,
though I'm thankful animals are spared. The Dalai Lama

himself would have appreciated my calm that afternoon.
Walking into that room to sit across from you at that table,

months after my birthday, you smiling at me like we'd just
met: perhaps it was true. We had only just met.

There was a reason for language back then. Back then,
words meant something. I am bent down, kneeling to pick

up the bouquet you've sent that's been left by a delivery
person employed to get its message received. Across our

table, my tears are not diamonds, nor does the sun's knife
come off my smile. Remember when your floor met my knees?

You're lucky I'm as lazy as I am. Animals like me, knives like
me, strange as forgiveness. I picked those bad flowers up.

Against Daylilies

Parking lot perennial. Predictable serial killer.
Your gladness peoples the concrete corners
of big-box shops as you sit, stalwart, atop

the gritty digs in which your tubers finger
sad dirt for nutrients, your orange mouths
open their baby-bird craws, suck up exhaust

as shopping carts racket by windowless vans.
I don't like how I dig you up again and again
but fail to grasp all your knotty bits that seem

to have found it in their will to sprout again.
I did what the gardening center man said
I should do to you, threw you into a roadside

ditch where he promised no one would spy
your flames, where no drive-by audience would
bother to ogle those baubles you call petals.

To think I used to serve you up in the vase
I place at the center of my table, loving how you
managed to dial up suns in nowhere zones;

to think I used to eat breakfast within inches
of your scent, speckled and tigery-breathed.
But I've smoked so long I can no longer feel

the effect of your musk breath, and I can eat
the color orange in an egg, and eat any man's
peculiar stare by closing my eye on it like

a mouth. The most interesting thing about
Ted Bundy, in my opinion, is that he was so
boring journalists came to dread talking to him.

Friendship Ghazal

You can't hold on to everybody like a bag of grapes won't promise
every grape is attached to the vine: I should know not all friendships

prove their promise of wine after the party, or letters that will feel
their way, miraculous, into the mailbox years later. Sure, friends

fall out, fall off, discreet in their nudges toward the darker ends of
hallways. I've done it myself, dropped the letter into the slot, shipped

it off with no return address. Easy on the sender. Nowadays we call
it *ghosting*, which is oddly clean in meaning in that it suggests friends

who abandon us on doorsteps will return to haunt us, though never
in the actual flesh. Years later, I'm desperate enough to try to refriend

you on Facebook on my phone, walking off a red-eye into the sunrise.
You have not disappeared entirely, jot off a response to say, *No shit!*

I'll be in touch soon! Remember when I set you up with my friend? You
told me she asked you to come on her face. *Who does that kind of shit,*

I wondered, when I should have asked why you were telling me that
shit; moreover, why would you humiliate a woman your old friend

set you up with by leaving her at a train station three hours before
her departure? Why did her predicament feel unsettlingly familiar?

You paid the bill so you could choose the restaurant. You always drove.
Don't support the hypothesis that women prefer to be treated like shit.

It's funny, I think I was the first, the last, certainly the only one: I must
have been the only woman with whom you were ever actually friends.

I don't dangle like a modifier. I hang in the air all these years later, fog up your windowpane with my breath. It's me, Marvin, your old friend.

War on Fun

In a deceitful time with a deceitful friend
I stayed at sea for days called *sea days*
on a vessel with casinos for hallways
as triumphant waves licked the ship's
sides in blackest night and luscious wet

bodies leapt to smack balls over nets
on the pool deck. It was my birthday
and poor cell-phone service disguised
the lack of a call or text from a man
I longed back then to call *my boyfriend.*

I drank in Dazzles, a lounge like a theater
that morphed from dance party to game
show within an hour, ordering double
whiskeys by the dozens, the bill accruing
invisibly, almost like a portent, a receipt

unspooling into the fathoms of a sky
that seemed to move its length like a giant
cat alongside the wind and water whipping
up at me from the deck side where I stood
smoking one cigarette after another.

My dreadful friend, latent back then
like a disease, claimed seasickness, chewed
on Dramamine, cluttered our berth
with products designed to make her privates
hygienic, worthy, chemical, or, as she

said, because she was *so sensitive down
there.* The only reason I was on that ship

was due to a conflict between her and her
rehab friend, who cut her off after the fatal
discovery of stolen pills. This friend

had booked the trip for her birthday,
and my birthday happened to be one
day after, the all-costs-paid trip was a mere
$400, so I thought I may as well experience
it, the lower-level art gallery with art so

ugly it stood in direct opposition to
notions of art, and what I was doing there
was due to my being in a weak position: I was
lonely. The purpose of the journey, it soon
became apparent, was to experience *fun,*

which was doled out in many formulas
and flavors, none of which agreed with me.
It was, I saw, a metaphor for the life I had
not yet lived and avert at every corner
I turn: a friend whose sleep is malicious,

who concocts tales of having once seen
a ghost in your attic, which is described
unremarkably as donned in a long white
nightgown, a candlestick clutched in her
hands, her hair wild and white. Was that

me, wandering my attic, just above my
own head? I'm not the medium, I have
no funnel to prop open to the essence
of the other world. I failed to distinguish
between a friend who is devoted to me

and the friend now approaching as I stand
by the railing, smoking, pouring myself
into the task of regarding the voluminous
carpet of the sea, her hand gentle at my
back. On those sea days and nights how

she smiled, as she smiled at me often,
watching me trip and tasting my shoe on
the step in the back of her throat. Now
that I have experienced so much intentional
fun, I have given up on fun, now that

this venal friend has made her apology
years after, I do not accept. I do not
accept fun, the fun that is for liars,
peering down and over the ship's side
from which hundreds of lifeboats hung.

It's a Limousine

It is nothing like a shark but the monochrome blanched off-white
of its long body is dumb like a shark's nose and dead eyes and
it is turning a corner.

                There's always a child in awe who asks
what is that. And we must supply the information, however
embarrassing our world may be in the explanation.

                              For example
this dumb automobile that will make me one day explain Prom,
which made me, personally, throw up in a parking lot. Or wealth.
That one is difficult.

                Because the sparkling wide-eyed young ones
all want all the money and candy and most especially baby kittens
the size of gumdrops that will never grow up.

                        For them our world
is a cotton-candy haze except when you accidentally mention
a dead cat who was named "Peanut." Then the storm appears
on the brow, looms like charred

                        coffee at the depths of a cup.
And why shouldn't we give that man bent on the corner money?
(Because we don't have much money, honey.) What's that?
A man who drives a very nice car

                    and is just about to hit you. You must
remind these little dum-dums they are very small, no one can
see them, anyone is liable to run them over, no one cares about
what grade

          they're in, they must stop touching everything,
they can't have cake, popcorn, Popsicles, cupcakes for breakfast,
lunch, or dinner. It's a limousine, and it represents every stupidity
known to human

           kind. And you, my child, are never allowed to ride
in one. May they one day become obsolete, may spaceships replace

them, may you one day cease to force me to answer all of your questions about this

                    awful world again. Though by then I may be dead. And for now I'll take grabbing your hand in mine while crossing this fearsome parking lot as my one true reason to live.

Lindens

While walking the dog I want nothing to do with
along the bend of a cove that cusps salt marsh, it

feels far too early to be awake. The air does not
serve the nose a single spoonful of salt but wafts

belligerently first sweat then sugar. Lindens
laden with the scent of honey and semen. Charlie

always moves eagerly in his greetings, needing
his nose to arrive at knees and groins, he barrels

toward any piss-scented weed, so we lurch, start
again, and often, I often curse at him. I used to love

the smells the lindens gave off; they'd pitch me
into recollection. I even sometimes stuffed petals

into my pockets to share with my husband once
I got home, though I always forgot, later pulling

crumbling petals out of those pockets, pitching the
pants into the washing machine. Charlie used

to be my least preoccupying household concern,
but now I appreciate how he launches me down

the streets, because he and I are alone together.
Even though he tugged me down the stairs that

time I twisted my ankle. I hated him back then,
lying on my back on the sidewalk, as he panted

above me. He was 80 pounds then. Now he's 70.
He cries with joy when I come home nowadays,

and if there is a heaven it will involve me lying
beneath covers on a bed and Charlie curled next

to me. Later this week, I'll get Charlie trimmed.
I like to have his rangy coat made clean so I can

see his shape, make sure he's not getting fat. It's
not vanity: weight hurts the joints on a dog big

as that. All tonight, I ignored Charlie, after I had
walked with him three miles down Washington

Ave., him striding ahead of me, as if all of this were
his idea; I forgot he existed because I got caught

up in looking up a gravesite on the Find a Grave
website, because there was her name, carefully

etched, on a piece of rose-colored marble. I like
walking Charlie beneath the row of lindens that

line the Back Cove, because there is no destination,
because people leave water bowls for dogs like

him by the water fountains. Because Charlie will
never kill himself, nor has he the intelligence to

betray me. Charlie just is. Charlie is a dog, that's
all. My friend's grave proves one of two things:

she would have been better off as a dog, or she
should have been a better dog. Tomorrow, when

I go to walk Charlie beneath those fragrant lindens,
I shall try much harder to not think of these things.

Blue

for Adam Zagajewski (1945–2021)

I really like that joe-pye weed.
Pictures of pretty pink wildflowers
can hinder sorrow for a second,
by the idea of filling my yard with
the distraction of blossoms whose
colors turn on like a hundred radio
stations all at once. The problem
with plants for me is all the names
I can't remember. The Latin names

will defeat me. I can't grasp all those
syllables. I don't want to live this
way anymore, adjacent to a pain
that operates at such a high frequency
it ruins my nerves, insisting I forget
that which is important to me like all
the colors that are possible, which is
why I always resent the question
What is your favorite color when

trying to retrieve a password when
locked out of an account and I have
forgotten the answer I gave the day
I set up that security question: Did I
choose blue or had I thought (again)
that there just are too many blues to
describe and how I like not all of them
but most, most especially the one right
at the tip of dawn, which pours its

crazy syrup of sorrow into your eyes
and makes you think longing is all
this life ought to be about, springing
your nerves into sleep after a long
night's work, the color of eyes that
refuse to blink, the color of eyes
destroying themselves with sorrow.
The blood slows. Syrup in the veins.
Driving to the grocery store. Many

times I thought to write him, these
letters in my head alive with delight
and gratitude. But failed to. What was
I doing? The moment he slipped into
the ether: Exercise class? Napping?
Conversing with a seashell? Installing
new locks on my doors? I said I don't
want to live this way anymore. Sweet
joe-pye weed is exactly what I need,

its *gravelroot, trumpetweed, feverweed.*
Its kidney root, feathery heads, fibrous
stalks. Its dominion and its nativity.
I'm not from anywhere, I once lied. Or
did I say red? I would never answer
orange though my secret truth is it's
actually my favorite color. You'd notice
if you sat in my living room. It's subtle,
Adam, but it's threaded in everywhere.

Narcan

It is not unusual to walk by someone who has fallen
down on the sidewalk and appears dead. Your brother
went like that back in the '90s. Slung over with hands

limp and pants falling, a man, young, gets public with
his slumber on the college campus. He's bent against
the steps. Knees splayed. Face closed. He must be tired,

work and schoolwork on top of work, I assume, when
my student fixes her eyes on mine with fervor, explains
she's followed MLA guidelines, for she is now all about

earning good grades as a mother of two, and her eyes
are glistening with fatigue and the glamour of tasting
her own excellence after taking apart the Blake poem

and fighting for his vision of chimney sweepers. She
speaks so fast I can hardly understand her as campus
police approach us, so I stomp out my cigarette, fearful

they'll scold me for smoking on the smoke-free campus.
Instead they move around me toward the man asleep
against the steps, ask him is he okay as if speaking to

a child. They jar his body and his eyes open a bit. His
pants fall low so his pale stomach shows, and his eye-
jellies roll and his mouth dumb-wide starts to move

around some words. Now, I move my student past him,
past her succinct terror regarding the next assignment
and its instructions. We are rising like clouds up these

stairs into this building, and now we are heading down some stairs to settle into our chairs and hours. We are turning this basement classroom into our heaven. We

look each other in the eyes. I remember your brother.

Anime Eyes at Corners

The neighborhood my father would have called *undesirable*
      is the neighborhood I live in,
having always preferred being between *here* and *there.* One
      drives slowly to prevent
possibly swiping the old white man with low pants who could
      be described as *traipsing*
by the food pantry. I still feel my own mother installed in me
      like a GPS. Each person
standing at these corners feels to me dangerous. *Who is their*
      mother? I wonder. For
everyone has a mother. I fear my child will ask this question:
      Where do they sleep?
How do I explain. I do not know where. In parks? She will fold
      for them origami beds
out of small delicious squares of paper. Or she may not look up,
      being too intent drawing
cat faces, faces that construct a fantasy of fluff and pink noses,
      their wide eyes' luster
depicted by two symmetrical ovals drawn inside their pupils.
      These cats look out at us
as if regarding us most spectacular creatures from their moon
      thrones, their feline planet,
which is the world in which my child resides, which means she
      is like her mother and
resides in her head, which is our curse. My serial cat-sketcher
      whose head hosts only
concerns regarding the habits of cats makes designs delicious-
      strange. Looking into their
spectral eyes is like eating a sugar cookie on the moon, or seeing
      what it might feel like to be
conceived of as a star, and it is also an opportunity to experience
      the persistence of a vision.

Caramel, glitter, moisture. *Forever* glints in the goo of loving eyes,
       a sticky glance trapped
in the amber of a moment. *Stay.* She will not remember a certain
       jagged window in the house
with a crooked fireplace and how one day we rolled our suitcase
       out to the car and drove
away. Everyone's mother wants to see her child safe. Do not lurch,
       do not move between
traffic as dirigible, cast your body in apathetic sway before these
       air-conditioned cars
that cocoon us, our glassy eyes always set upon the specter
       of this world as if
we are watching a gourmet dish being prepared on television.
       Toss in yourself and mix
it up. The world is the oven we bake in, only to deliver ourselves
       to the mouths of our lovers,
to ourselves becoming mothers, mother of this: There is no love
       larger than these eyes
filling notebooks. They are in fact the child's craft, their shading,
       her making. *Far be it from*
me to ask her to look up now! But I must ask her to look up now.
       She looks up. She sees.

In the Future a Robot Will Take Your Job

It's not my job to make you happy though
it was my job to make my last husband happy

despite the fact I was paying him through the nose
with my student loans and sending him swan

bouquets at great expense, their intricately
lettered placards pleading *Please don't hit me*

again. I still can't stop smoking. Sometimes
it feels like I'm standing on that back porch

staring out at the lawn from my middle-aged
face, squinting into all the gray hair looking

back at me from the clouds of my future: I am
bones. Bones crack inside a body like glass

in a sack, rattle shards against the dresser
drawers after a body is flung from

a bed. He'd been laid off. The toll this took
made his face undertake a dance of tremors:

one eye atwitch blinked, the other winked,
stuck on its lie like a typewriter key stuck on

a letter. Now he is asleep. Darkness seeps
from out the room into the hall. Hands press

air to meet the bed, feel it out in the soft black.
Now I fold myself beside him: dreams wait

on lavender cusps of cloud-breeding gods—
then two hands sudden press, elbow edges

jangle, my tailbone landing hard on wood.
Why not just go ahead and fashion my coccyx

into a key chain? Stop blaming the economy.
Who pays for husbands anyway? Mine needed

a job not to hit me. He lost his job. Then there
were no jobs. In the future a robot will take his job.

It would take a robot to make him happy.
It will take a robot to make his robot happy.

Violets

The way some people are about weeds: I'm not
as forgiving. I see a weed and could will a knife

out my eyes to gouge its root. It has no place in
my garden, which means it can go anywhere it

likes, but it'd be better off counting this flower
bed out. I love to think while weeding, and I do

so meticulously. I think of everyone who has
ever crossed me, I cross the sea of ex-husbands,

I reimagine my dowry and regard suitors once
worthy who are now shackled to others. Why,

I wonder, was I so cruel, as I jab the trowel in
deeper, press fingers along the root's length

to be certain I've got it all, that it'll never come
back. I toss the tangle onto the tarry drive to

bake distant from its source. That's our glad
friend the dandelion, which my daughter so

sweetly hands me, which I see as an evil star
with jagged fronds outspread exactly where I

don't want, which is everywhere. I'm almost
fond of that plant, though I'll never consider

eating its greens (let's not pretend), compared
to how I feel about violets, so grotesque with

their rhizomes that are sometimes larger than
the as-yet-unrealized ambitions of their leaves.

Violets are possessed of a skank sneakiness
that, after reading about it and then taking

apart the plant to fully examine it, recognize
its design, stunned me: the sprightly purple

of its face masquerades as propagator while
ghostly droplets of seeds flourish beneath

the umbrellas of leaves, so close to the earth
they are practically buried, nursing the soil

with their paleness. It's pure Hades. My love
said, standing at the kitchen sink, *Why does it*

seem you want to destroy every plant I love?
First it's violets, now daylilies. How could I

have known their strange, their orange, their
staggered roadside stems, reminded him of

his dead friend, signaling the ghost memory
of them white-water rafting on the Allagash?

He was aghast. But how did the two connect?
I'm not sure. This friend poured himself down

a sink, departing into the underworld, his last
guided trip down the sweet Lethe. They call

them ditch lilies. Which is where I threw them.
Must I sacrifice my aesthetics for sentiment?

You think I discriminate. I admit that so many
tubers, the nubby handfuls of them, along with

their audacity to grow anywhere, got to me.
I began to think it gross. In my defense, we

had a hard winter. How many of the flowers
I planted will I see again? No matter. I refuse

to beg them to turn their faces toward the sun.
I myself have lost almost everyone. Some plants

I'd plant again, others I'd forgo. I don't know.
Whisper greeny nudges to plants you love all

you like, say *It's safe to come out now.* But that's
not true. That's not true at all. Gimme a break.

Virus

For once I considered the manner in which the breeze
lifted the leaves that had died to gather in the roadside

ditch by the mailbox reminiscent of your hair beneath
the rake of my fingers. Your pelt like a wolf curled hot

in sleep all winter, dumb and luxurious as I imagined
your mind, envying the proximity of your body to hers

as one who stands freezing in a bus depot eyes coats
that ride the bodies pressing toward the heat pooling

out from the station's careless doors. And now, at last,
but long after I have ceased to care, the germs arrive

to align our lives. Who will cough first? Who between
us will carry the virus silently, unwitting accomplice?

You first met me diseased, admired my pockmarks.
I turned my face from you, walked back to my sickbed.

Is that how you came to admire me? The word of your
handsomeness had always traveled a few days ahead

of you, a royal emissary. Was it that I was preoccupied
by a pestilence receding, its fever finishing its last lap

through my veins? You will mistook my illness for
nonchalance. I was the first woman to rise from a bed

and approach you with sores. And this is how I make
the first of several mistakes: I heal. Ultimately, I find

your flaws in your language. Flourishes rise from your
letters like something ripe. It is you to whom I credit

starting me off on this long journey of feeling nothing.
Which of us will die first? Who will infect the populace?

I wish I'd never met you is beside the point. Had we
never met, I wouldn't have come so far with my well-

regarded study of dismay. You'd be a better person if
someone had been considerate enough to scar your face.

Starfuckers

Beer Lotto Wine Cigs is a sign before a door-
way I walk through to buy a bottle of water,
is a hole I fall some stairs down into in order
to buy a bottle of water for three dollars from

a shop that features two old men sitting in
their dirt by the register and who laugh at
charging me a dollar for a banana; I'm sure
they'll have lots to joke about once I turn to

walk back out, cross the street to climb back
up to the room in which I am thinking about
Leda and the Swan and what I can't get over
is how the search results always direct me

to the same object of focus: I am wondering
how it would feel to travel down a swan's
throat as a water reed, and if the fluid neck's
vertebrae are not unlike a snake's, and is there

a coiling that a swan undertakes should it wish
to be your companion, say, weaving its neck
around your arm thrice before tucking its head
to rest beneath your breast? The search terms

for *swan swallowing* allow me to consider that
the words reversed mean to suck a penis, and
just below, there is a video of Two Happy Swans
Eating Lunch. Would Marianne Moore not have

adored the internet? She was never one of those
girls who made goo-goo eyes at guys, she never
traipsed late night the grounds of some writers'
conference, never slipped out from the poet's

room; instead she was counting her fragments,
fossils, filaments and syllables under her own
bright light recklessly and methodically as old
Chinese women go at mah-jongg in the park; she

was wise in that she was always only about her
art. She didn't herself get mixed up in a domestic
situation, no man ever grabbed her by the neck
because she insisted he turn his music down,

the baby is sleeping. She solved that problem
before it could start by having no babies, no
men, allowing only her preoccupation with
craft to balloon itself up inside the room of her

life, her attraction to chintz china *vital and fatal*
as one critic closed her piece like a beak. I think
I rarely think of Moore, but realize I must think
more of Moore than I realize. She had no messy

umbrage. But she, like Leda, sat on wonders, no
doubt. She could not have pretended not to, not
now in our age of sex videos and selfies. Hands
feel like rubber on the neck that holds the head

up screaming to turn the music down because
the baby is sleeping. The neck feels the hands
as if they were not attached to the man. Hands,
however, do not have brains, do not arrive upon

one's throat of their own accord. It's not the swan
that is violent, nor is it the man; rather this brand
of excitement is the liberty of gods. Yeats's version
is all over the police blotter, but I wonder which

is worse depicted: force or coercion? The swan
in so many pictures poses as a companion, a pet,
or, in one, an amateur gynecologist who peers curious
between the splayed legs of a woman supine, as

if prepared to use its beak as a forceps. Bishop
is another one who probably saw such images
and, restrained as she was, made the decision
to make no mention of it. The thought of some

god disguised as a swan shimmying up to me makes
me nauseous. God posing as a sort of arm candy.
My daughter's favorite purse, silver with a small
swan, the notions crawl out manholes to reach

for my ankles just before I step into the store
in which I buy my bottle of water from the old
men. They appear unwashed, the kind of old men
we consider *abandoned,* luckless, spent, no kind

and grateful women to look after them. Their
table is covered with cards and bills and whirls
with their laughter shared like lovers'. The store
offers more more more of what I really do want:

wine and cigarettes, but my brain is ailing me
and I cannot recall which night I lasted late,
slipped inside a pine tree to hide and pretend
I was not one of those girls. I got lost the second

his hand appeared on my knee. What were those
girls looking for, I'd wonder; we used to call them
Starfuckers, when all they wanted was to close
the gap between teacher and student, god and

mortal, all those swans walking around smoking
their own poems! The Ledas wanted what they
got, so it seemed to me as I walked buckling over
drunk back to my room. These old men must be

successful selling three-dollar bottles of water
to parched drunks just flush from lotto winnings;
only in that state of delirium would a reasonable
human frequent this store. It has everything I want

and nothing I want anymore. I don't drink anymore,
but I can't say I don't cry anymore. I cry more!
Maybe I was a sort of starfucker, too, inside that
conifer, thinking myself a little god disguised

behind needle and sap, too good for the regular
fucking of people enjoying an evening, taking
things, as usual, too seriously, unable, as always,
to just *relax.* It's weird to me to think that I still

have the body I had then now. All its digits are
intact. The problem with the story is the binary
nature of the interpretation: it was either rape
or pleasure. Neither equation fails to surprise

or repulse me. The pair of hands that grabbed
my neck are a hundred towns back, the baby
a girl who sees the flimsy literalness of a myth.
And the girl I was is still in the pines, maybe,

lurking and turning into her own weird swan
of that swamp, chucking up weeds dredged
from the silty deep to tug them down the long
trail of throat, miles and miles, its dark-supple

eternity where all the ghosts go, even the girls
who hated me as I hated them, despite being
poets too: I realize now, we were all Ledas,
all our tongues were all stretched and pulled

deep inside that swan's dark belly. I thought
to wipe Moore right out of this poem, until my
own mother on the phone, listening as mothers
do, sighed, *Oh, the one who wore the tricorn.*

Blue Lights

The night classes pour into asphalt lots
that soon empty of their engines,
the students seeming to dissolve like raindrops,
the students seeming now to have been a hallucination

that buzzed angrily for hours beneath fluorescent-lit
ceilings at poems like hands that refused to be held
or glittered their eyes at the kisses placed by
poems on their palms, longing for the vantage

of multiple-choice answers over these overtures
of beauty and malignance. And the question
not just once but again, again, *What is it?*
They are all gone, the poems and their students,

have left me to wander into this mist settling
across the soft lawns this nether time of night,
to walk solitary toward my car's lone smudge beneath
the morose lumens cast from corners of campus

that have stationed at them lighted poles that
glow a chlorine blue, designated lightning rods for fear,
bedecked with alarm buttons to run to for
pressing, to send sirens out to saviors.

When did these lighted poles appear, their beacons
utterly unreachable? Even spied from behind
the windshield, one apprehends a great distance
between their stars and the bus stop's canopy,

beneath which hooded students smoke only
to disappear into the damp exhaustion of the night.
Which is always when the deer appear, ornament
themselves upon the lawns, frozen in mist,

taking on the stance of the startled, now startlingly
pale, the four before me equidistant, and one
tipping the pitcher of her head as if to pour the grass
a drink or, considered upside down, suckle the milk

from soil or nurse the grass's dew. My bag of books
thrown over my back like a bag of bones, my bag
of poems a bag of stones, crushes my shoulder
as I wade in mist toward the car, and the deer,

who watch me as I watch them, seem a dream's
decision to find me far outside the room I sleep in.
They are an astonishment I do not wish to analyze.
And I am certain if I move too quickly they will, spooked,

run from me, or I am scared that if I do not run from them
they will stampede the meagerness that is me.
The buck tumbling before my headlights.
The scrimp of lawn in the mouth of the doe.

Sunbathers

I wake up in the sun by the lake on sand that
scorches the feet that lie like little dead fishes
at the ends of my legs. I lie like a dead thing

alongside the blankets and picnic baskets of
strangers who scorch meat they did not slaughter
on coals they do not coax but douse with liquid

that flames huge at the mere touch of a match.
I am in New England, and my blood is nearly
one-half English, I recently learned from a DNA

test kit, and I am one of those white people who
lies on sand, who lies all the time, who lies to herself,
who can write about feeling dead on a beach but

never worry about being dead really, only employ
the poem to rhapsodize about an idea of death.
I'm afraid all the time in Maine, but not because

someone's going to go after me. I'm a tourist of
another's danger. It's not my worry, but I worry.
There's got to be a moral in this. My neck will never

know a knee, is just one example. A body's heft
set down upon a knee on a neck. A neck's fragility
beneath a knee! I cannot stand to see the TV, its

empty, frozen fuckery. Sometimes I feel my feet
are set in concrete blocks by a villain in preparation
to drop me to this lake's bottom, sink me forever.

It seems certain—I see my white self there. In concrete,
my dead white feet are the whitest things ever. I'd
chop them off if they weren't what makes me walk.

Friend of the Flies

My weirdling child indentures herself to collecting
sticks in something called a garden
that is barely a garden yet full of flies. Watching
her from up high, my head stuck out
a window's frame, I see no great violation's taken place.
She is merely industrious, stockpiling
the many thin reeds she calls *flutes* on a wrought-iron

patio table; her piles are neat. It's the flies she's faithful
to. She strokes their wings, makes
this space a space that she insists is a home for them.
They are, she insists, her friends,
and she is eager to get back to them, she explains while
taking a break to spoon soup up
to her lips, her dirt-furrowed brow tensing kitchen air.

I need to be out there. So down the stairs she goes again,
gone for some hours. I recall that
afternoon I was lessoned on how to ground a winged ant
that had landed on the bench on
which we sat when she stopped to rest after I watched
her shaky progress down a path
on new Rollerblades, and she asked, as if offering a glass

of iced tea, did I want her to "ground" the creature? What
did she mean? The ant? *Yes, you
pull off its wings,* she says. *That's what grounding means,*
she replies cheerfully. I ask her,
*How might YOU feel if some larger being leaned down, pulled
your arms off?* Then she laughs.
The friend of flies has had a good afternoon. Now she lies

like a very small queen so dead asleep, mouth puffed ajar,
the tooth that is constantly one
second from being lost clanking in the wind of her baby
breath. Tomorrow some anthill
will find itself the object of grave misfortune as my daughter
will see to save it, gather stones
to surround it to prevent the onslaught of rain or a terrible

boy-rival's hands. *Don't touch that,* I'm always saying. *Don't
touch that.* And then she pushes her
hand (her nails never moons, her slivers black, crudded up
with grime) into my large hand which
receives hers as ocean anemones allow sunfish to swim among
their tendrils. So as to feel the softness
of her small fingers. For O how I love my friend of the flies.

Walking Around a Lake

When we move ourselves around its edge like a thread,
circumvent it, is it like we are enclosing it over and over
again, remaking the lake, enforcing the lake's shape, as

a finger knows its ring, as a ring takes its place on a digit
and makes its claim? Do you too fear a ring's constriction?
Are we not always the same, our two figures circling fate,

a fate that lies atop a pile of fates aboard a boat always
afloat at the center of a lake while we joke about crawling
through the eelgrass at night to shoot a hole in its hull?

The sun is setting its plate on the sky's table. We would
lick the skin off each other with our eyes. Now tell me as
I shake, how deep do you think is the middle of the lake?

How do charts differ from maps, what god-finger sinks
to dip its digit, press at the bottom, pliable and soft, mud
tender, to learn where water stops and the lake bed starts?

In New Mexico

I liked you better when you were fat. Your stare still makes me
feel like a nerve is going off behind your eyes, an alarm I can't hear.

Over the years I've never been able to unfasten from your mouth
what transgression made you turn your face from me, disappear.

We meet at a restaurant you've chosen, the unspoken agreement
you'll pay and I should order at my leisure. Why do I even care?

That's a good question. One I've been ignoring. In New Mexico,
you've acquired the same kind of friends you always keep near.

One joins us for dinner, a younger musician; you pay for his meal
too. When he comes back to your townhouse with us, it's clear

he'll stay long after I leave. You show me your dead cat's pelt.
It feels just like the cat who wound around my ankles, appeared

next to me when I woke up on your couch. Remember how
you used to call a cat psychic who had a unique ability to hear

what animals thought? It was after you were forced to abandon
this particular cat. She relayed its singular message: *When are*

you coming back? You hold its skull out on your palm. You say
a specialist in the desert boiled the head down to this bone-nut.

You don't offer to drive me back so I have to find my way out
of a neighborhood I don't know in the dark, my phone steering

me in the direction of my hotel. I came here by myself to do
a poetry reading. It became an excuse to look you up. Here

I am again, moving through the dark. Christ, you would think
I'd never lost a friend before. Back at the hotel room, I swear

I'll never see you again. Forlorn (*the word is like a bell*) is how
I feel. But then I think of how you treated your cat and sneer.

My Father's Liquor Cabinet

They'll try and keep anyone alive, doctors. They
split him in half, combed him for tumors, fished

nodes out to pry open their bad cells. He wasn't
happy when he woke up, despite the surgery

having been a "success." You'd almost feel sorry
for him, move closer to the rustle of his hospital

gown, lean over and

                this reminds the psychologist
of the fable in which the lion plays feeble as his

teeth are dull, inviting his friends to pay their
last respects. They succumb, only the fox spying

the paw prints in dust outside the lair, only
going in and never out. It's a worn-out tale but

                the night I was shot
from his seed into Mother and I came whistling

through a passage with my needles of noise as
if to erect a column of days positioned like bars,

a winter's prism, a scorpion. Still I must crouch
at a distance. Like the fox did,

the psychologist says.
Outside his lair. Though he might be toothless—

when I was solar and spasm, he pushed himself
into the body of my mother and a kinetic ease

overcame him as he dropped forward to rest
his forehead hard against

at the dentist

I am arguing on behalf of my teeth: they have
been in my mouth so long you cannot expect

them to be straight, you can't ask anything of
them for all the candies they chewed, the lies

that have ground their molars down, wearied
my fangs

while snowed up in my
mother's uterus, my coin purse heavy with ill

wishes, I paced the floors of a house half glass,
its windows tacked straight up from the breathy

bottom of a forest where a stream once sprung,
but which is now paved over, he said

he's sewn up from his
groin to his throat. He's no longer even capable

of being mean when that was always what he
was so good at: he hated animals and adored

machines. I'm all animal and anti machine.
One of his tubes has slipped out of his gown,

is leaking onto the floor

                          his head sinks back within
the frame, as a water moccasin withdraws

into its swamp. But wait. His head is oddly
perched, as if every little sapling that ever

grew in him was stomped. He's since bought
a cemetery plot

                          he lurches beneath August
sun before the church fair's offerings of jarred

dilly beans, junked air conditioners, fastidiously
kept sets of glassware, totters toward an awning

erected above the shining skins that cap the pale
heads of pale old men

                          and there's room for me too,
should I choose to be cremated: in grave plots

urns fit neatly in corners. He hated animals.
He recited Eliot's "Hollow Men" at the dinner table.

I see no evidence that God exists. You can choose what you want to believe when you grow up.

Days of 1994

That was the year *depression* first began appearing on billboards.
I read the advertisement as a pharmaceutical ploy to ease the bills

from out my wallet. Making $10 an hour typing up medical reports,
I spent each day in a cubicle wincing beneath fluorescence, bored,

sure, but paying my rent. How else could I afford spending night
after night at the Grand Tavern? I couldn't really. You paid the bill.

Tumblers of Bloody Marys chunky enough to count as a meal, crisp
celery stalks staking the icy heart of the glass, strong enough to bore

several holes in one's ambitions, its lip dusted with Old Bay. Back
then, I cried all the time. You dropped that you were getting *bored*

with me always complaining that I was tired. I didn't have the balls
to mention a check I'd seen on your dresser from your mother made

out for more than I made in a year. *Depression.* The thought of taking
mind medicine was unthinkable: it might knock down all I'd built

out of words with the blueprints of tears. Take your Welch and this
question: Why is every book on your bookshelf written by a man?

But sometimes I wish myself back there with you right now to lick
that glass's lip's edge for its salt. What did I have to complain about?

Now I take 10 mg Lexapro daily for anxiety. And pop Klonopin for
panic episodes. Self-medicate with vodka seltzers for mania. Bill

me for the hours you listened to my plight, my dreams of vengeance.
You can take your Whalen, your bookshelf overlords: B-O-R-I-N-G.

It's taken me forever to give up on you. Now take your medicine.
You'll find Willa Cather in the library. She's not in your collection.

The Maine Motel

I

Once I called that motel and let the phone ring and ring
and no one ever answered. I dialed again and let it ring

Room 24 some more, hoping to hook a woman named
Barbara on my line's end. I'd kept a small piece of paper

folded into a square inside my wallet, and I unfolded it
again to read the neatly penciled letters to make sure

I'd made no mistake. But it was impossible to mistake
the name Barbara for another or Room 24 for another

room. Clarity in penmanship of the young reveals the
kind of pained effort particular to a small hand new to

the rigors that numerals require. When I looked up the
address for the motel, its number matched the number

on that piece of paper.
                              Children's birthday parties.
I'm determined to snag this Barbara's voice from out

from the well of the dial tone, lob the lasso of my voice
into Room 24 to offer my assurance I am *a mother she*

can trust. Barbara's son is now waving goodbye to my
daughter as the yellow buses tug themselves away from

curbsides, force the day to depart from itself. Barbara?

II

The Maine Motel is shutting down.
Its blackened eyes close at last
on the alley it's long batted its lashes
at. Women who are mothers stand
with signs at intersections I drive
through. *Please help anything counts.*
I am a mother who keeps her
windows rolled up. I drive past

the Maine Motel. The article calmly
states *residents may have heard
police use flash bang grenades.*
I keep reading it over, wonder
what warrants a display of *bright
light and thunderous blast.* Was
Barbara in one of those rooms?
If Barbara answered the phone,

what would I tell her? That I'm
not the kind of mother who'd dare
pack a peanut-butter sandwich
in her daughter's lunch box for
fear of contaminating the school
cafeteria's nut-free zone? Alone,
I crouch on my back steps, swirl
the air with cigarette smoke from

my lungs, press against a thought
solid as the glass behind which my
daughter rests: the free groceries
in brown bags handed out on Fridays,
by the buses. Fuck *nuts!* Only a long
time later will your kid confide she
knew her best friend back then did
not get to eat over the weekends.

III

You can lie in bed and pretend you can't hear
the wind breaking around the house. You can.

Some people can't. Some people can't sleep
on planes. Can't sleep anywhere. Your problem

is you can sleep anywhere. Turn the world off.
Make it go away. You own all the days just like

that, and only by lowering your eyelids. What
power, to draw the curtains shut. Disappear.

IV

I used to unfold that piece of paper out of my wallet
every now and again to try again. Was it persistence?

Dutiful or vengeful? Was there a point of which I was
in pursuit? Did I simply want to see the mother's face?

There is nothing simple about the desire to uncover
a face, for below my plain face lies a gossipy hag who

wants to look inside your every closet, every medicine
cabinet, feel out the interiors of your well-worn shoes,

know your smell. It is not empathy, the dog that pulls
on this leash of inquiry, but desire to make of oneself

an imposition. The problem for me with God wasn't
that I couldn't see or smell him in the room, but that

I never believed he was there in the first place. He's
done nothing for the children who drew the pictures

on display in this classroom we parents tour on Back
to School Night. Barbara's a no-show. Barbara's child

has drawn a flower. My child's drawn a burning house
with a truck carrying people and animals away from

the flames. Her child draws a flower, mine a disaster.
Which one do you think sleeps better?

I'm still waiting for your answer.

My Mother Hangs Up

I can feel her mind panting.
She asks me to save the program.

I almost convinced her to fly
to New York to see the performance

with me, but her knee is stiff
and she can't manage stairs.

She asks me which dancers.
And you know how mothers

make us who we are and who
we aren't. I speak to her

every day to find out who
I am not. Walking through

a grocery store talking to my mother
about an interview I read with the man

who choreographed this ballet,
I say *I think I finally understand*

the connection between poetry and dance.
My mother is getting ready

for her doctor's appointment.
The tradition and its forms,

which I honor, *and the urge*
to make the art relevant

to a contemporary audience.
I say to my mother *I get that*

but hesitate before I say *as an artist.*
Am I taking myself too seriously,

like that time I got mad at her
for selling my typewriter at

a yard sale and dared exclaim
across a table at a restaurant

something about my *work?*
But it was my mother who bought

nosebleed seats for matinees
when she was twenty-four

and went by herself. She took
me to see Baryshnikov dance

when I was five. I fell asleep
sucking my thumb. I loved

to suck my thumb, watching
the light fall on my mother's face

as she sat rapt in the audience
until I knew she was a goner

and that I could suck without
worrying she'd swat my thumb

out my mouth. Which is why
I ended up with buckteeth

that needed to be corrected,
which is why I ended up

with so many habits that have
needed correcting *I fell asleep*

watching Baryshnikov so maybe
I just want her to know I saw

what she saw at age 24 after
having extracted herself from

a small town in Pennsylvania
that promised to trap her

like an insect in amber. My mother
is also trapped by my expectation

that she listen to me all the time.
What I find most compelling

about the dance is *the magnitude
of the exactitude.* Then my mother

hangs up. She must get dressed
for her appointment.   Mommy!

My clothes are worn-out.
Why are we always paying rent to the world?

How can you not see what these dancers do
without wondering:

Did they ever want to have a baby?
How old were they when they first orgasmed?

How do they split their bodies like wood out back?
How can they lay their bones down like lines?

Which relative do they dread calling on Sunday?
Does having a baby feel like bad math?

You want to know
why I hate everybody?

All the loud people who
should leave the library

which is for writers the stage
as it is for dancers the mind.

I think this is the moment
in the poem the dancers

would click their arms in unison,
shutter themselves shut like fans,

close unto themselves as petals
close. Like I need my mother

to get her sophisticate self out
of my mind, stop closing on

me and my mind all the time.
Because all artists need

(*my mother hangs up*)

to spread like lichen on bark,
to exist so subtly you must imagine

the volume knob is turned all the way down.
It's the discipline she'll never understand.

Like any mother, you love me too much.
Like any mother, you think you know me.

I am stacking my wood out back.
I am aiming my ax at its cracks.

Mother. Heartwood.
I *am* your bad math.

Fixing Things

It is true I despised my father, as it is true
my life has been easier since he died.
It is also true that he knew how to fix

anything and that he was utterly reliable.
I could call on him whenever I was fixing
up any space I lived in, when installing

a light fixture or switch or spackling a wall
to ready it for paint. In these exchanges,
he was supremely patient, careful to assess

the situation, explaining in the clearest
terms how I might approach the project
in order to achieve the most desirable result.

It's frustrating to not have him on the other
end of the phone when approaching the many
problems I've encountered in the house

I now live in. Problems were never really
problems, but ambitions revealed through
obstacles—we loved as a family to make

a thing perfect. After a hard day, I lay my
legs on this table my father refinished as
a favor to me, which is a tree sliced in half,

an old stump. I arrive here: I don't have to
worry anymore. He's never going to pick up
the phone. He got a vasectomy when I was

two. For whatever reason, he never liked
me. If I don't look out for myself, who will?
I appear aimless in hardware stores, still.

The Real Book

What is the appeal of jazz to a certain kind of white man? Face
it, something snags here, makes me query, is it not a bit fascist

considering the production, the source of pain, and the mode
of consumption? But, then, I never went through a jazz phase.

Consider for a minute why in this rare instance no women's
hands are overtly tending men's sensitive instruments. Faces

are funny, lips made sex-stuff when female, our skin malleable,
gloves to a fist, soft cloths sweetening intention's mallet. A face

is a most presumptuous act! Don't look back. White men who
love jazz are unconventional as a Garnet Hill catalogue. Face

it, James, it does the job of expressing yourself for yourself.
Horns screamed and droned all those nights we got shitfaced

in your apartment on Holly. Why must men quell the guttural
with esoteric explanation? To rationalize obsession, save face.

I lay on your couch, letting jazz seep into my ears, fold over
my head, pour down past my body as snow filled in the faces

of windows. You spun records, and we spilled vodka fizzes till
the sun crouched down to peer in at us like an error, its face.

I Am in the House and I Have the Key

As one passes a yolk between the cups of halved
shells, dropping its gold back and forth gingerly

to let the sac of it fall whole into a bowl—is it not
like how these bodies that once seemed pieces

of cutlery divided inside a drawer into which we
reach for the tools that allow our hands their

measured arc to lift this food to our mouths?
Or are these bodies cutlery in unison and sync?

For how they make me see the use of us in unison,
wonder at how all our bodies lie through nights

silent across nations, that these bodies could be
lifted as if by strings to become a joyous machine:

joy at seeing a body that falls along a body that falls
along a body as a fan opens to reveal tremendous

green-gray plates like wings. Their silvers bewilder,
as does this gift: to sit on an achingly gracious seat,

allowed to imagine I could reach into my own legs
as if they were balloons, fill my lungs with stars

and oxygen and love—bubble gum, tobacco, pipes,
rollercoaster rides inside a frame that's hung in

a museum—and I am the only person in the room.
Or is it like being young again, which I do not miss,

having beaten its notion back with my indifference,
until I forgot it so hard I can't think it up the way

I used to as I smoked my own brain into the dawn
in an attic apartment, and the man I was *in love*

with for years was plain as a bowl of canned soup
warmed up on a homey stove that now sits in some

junkyard rusting its brilliance. But even that dull
man still breathes, and his eyes are beautiful. I can

admit that I like colorful stones. But these bodies
that open and close like fans complicate everything

in the same way a pie just out of the oven suggests
through its scent *Just because there's only one of me*

doesn't mean you can't make more! Because it tastes
like the fruit that grows behind your eyes, and licks

the plumage plaited around your neck, that feathered
collar of iridescence you were gifted at birth: beauty.

And that is the whole point, really. *Forgive me the words*
I once uttered. It is the only point in being alive.

They / Them / Theirarchy

I

It didn't matter that my daughter turned into a son
and then back again into a flame and cut their hair
off and flew up into the sky with a burst of feathers
I'd use to dust away the cobwebs. Or that I'd taken

to dressing as the battered women's hotline, that
my stalker was trying to pretend we'd never stood
before that judge in Essex County who stated *There
is no reason you ever need to talk to her again,* instead

writing me an email as if we'd remained friends. Or
that the woman who ran the session on domestic
abuse said it only takes a minute of stopping oxygen from
getting to the brain to cause brain damage (*gestures,*

her hands grabbing at her throat on the Zoom screen).
I, too, have been strangled. Women's faces collect in
rows of chocolate-box squares on my laptop. Each
one may as well be me. We look back at one another.

II

I was curled up inside my own daughter waiting for
her to ask for a razor. She was getting to be that age.
Her fingernails were long and elegant as spoons, not
gnawed like mine. Her teeth I love a lot, yellow ivory

tablets behind plush lips. She'd inherited the nostrils
of my grandmother: they were tiny and imperious as
those of a hippopotamus. In fact the one prayer I'd
made was for her not to end up with this particular

nose. But when I saw it on her, I saw she pulled it
off. It was bitterly, cruelly cute, a challenge because
if her nose was stuffy folks could see right up it. She
was not a feminine daughter either, which suited me

better; she'd sliced the ice skates right off her ankles
and refused to dance. Her hands, however,
were almost unnaturally feminine, the digits slender,
nails tapered. It's the hands that will give them away.

III

My daughter is gone. She snuffed her name. It meant
light. I spent months thinking it up. When they were
four, the man I was with told me he thought my kid
had a *bad streak*. This coming from a blackout drunk

who spent his days looking out from his second-story
window, chain-smoking, casting terrible stares down
at me whenever I pulled into the driveway. They can't
remember any of this, nor the day I scooped them up

into my arms, put them in the car, and we drove away.
Perhaps it feels this way to them, like they are driving
away from something dangerous, their name. A name
becomes one's face. Sliding the wand, the nurse said

I think it's a girl. Now women's faces collect like tears
in a spoon. Who in their right mind wants to be poured
in along with them? We don't keep enough mirrors in
this house. They are more beautiful than they realize.

Acknowledgments

Much gratitude to the editors of the journals in which versions of these poems appeared:

Academy of American Poets Poem-a-Day: "Two Views of a Discarded Mattress"

The American Poetry Review: "Ice Cream in February," "Lottery of Eyes," and "You May Eat"

The Baffler: "It's a Limousine"

Bennington Review: "Narcan" and "Violets"

Birmingham Poetry Review: "My Father's Daughter" and "Rendezvous with Ghost"

Conduit: "Lindens"

Fence: "My Father's Liquor Cabinet," "My Mother Hangs Up," and "War on Fun"

Guesthouse: "Against Daylilies"

Harvard Review: "Blue" and "I Am in the House and I Have the Key"

Kenyon Review: "Event Horizon," "The Eyes of the Neighborhood," "Friend of the Flies," and "Starfuckers"

Narrative Magazine: "Days on 1994," "Friendship Ghazal," "In New Mexico," "The Real Book," and "Trying Too Hard"

New England Review: "Blue Lights" and "Faces"

Specific acknowledgments and dedications:

"Blue Lights" reads like it does thanks to the expert input of Erin Belieu.

In "The Eyes of the Neighborhood," the brilliant line *so shut up and take the grim future in your mouth* is the creation of Mykey Adme, my former student at the College of Staten Island. I extend gratitude to Mykey for allowing me to use it.

"Ice Cream in February" is for the poet Angela Williamson Emmert, my former student, whose amazing poem about eating Doritos in a parked car revealed to me how to rewrite this poem.

"Nostalgia Is A" is dedicated to Joe Dupont, with thanks for love and support over the years.

"Walking Around a Lake" is for Brenda from Cardiac Pacemakers, wherever she may be now.

The primary folks who got me through the making of this book are:

Katherine Larson, who helped me re-engineer just about every poem in this book and lifted my spirits whenever I felt like crud. She then got me across the finish line by providing fine-tuned final edits.

Colin Cheney and Jefferson Navicky, who were the first readers for nearly all of these poems. They pushed many of these poems far beyond their initial impulses, and I am deeply indebted for how much they have taught me.

Rick Barot, to whom I am deeply grateful for his unsparing insights into what's working and not working in my work.

Rebecca Wolff, who gave me many wise suggestions and edits when I was finishing this book.

Erin Belieu, whose intelligence astonishes, and whose kindness overwhelms.

Laurie Foos, my sister by another mother. "You know you can always . . ."

Special thanks to Laura Morra, for her gorgeous psychoanalytic chops.

Friends as necessary to me as the teeth in my mouth: Oona Adams, Adrian Blevins, Sarah Braunstein, Andy Brennan, Michael Dumanis, Bryn Grey, Wayne Johns, ZZ Packer, Megan Riggle, Aaron Sinift, Ann Townsend, Justin Tussing, Lauren Weinstein, Jonathan Wells, Jim Wyss, and Matthew Yeager.

For social and psychological support, I thank my Academics for Black Survival and Wellness accountability group members: Yulia Gilichinskaya, James Kim, Kathryn Newton, Elizabeth Severson-Irby, and Kara-Lynn Vaeni. Much love to the crew from Salud: Jess Howell, Polly Keniston, Dori Lewin, Paul Lewin, and Monica Wright. Deep thanks also to PFLAG of Portland, Maine.

I extend my deepest gratitude to Michael Wiegers and all the wonderfully supportive and contagiously passionate folks at Copper Canyon. Special thanks to Jessica Roeder, the fantastically thorough copyeditor Copper Canyon gifted me with. This book would not exist without gifts of time (which = money) from the Guggenheim Foundation, the Professional Staff Congress of the City University of New York, and the generous folks at the James Merrill House. Thanks also to all my colleagues in the English department at the College of Staten Island. I'm proud to work with you.

Every day is new thanks to my righteous child, Emerson Marvin.

And, finally, for her abiding support and great company, I thank Mary Jo Marvin, my mom and my best friend.

About the Author

Cate Marvin's first book, *World's Tallest Disaster*, was chosen by Robert Pinsky for the Kathryn A. Morton Prize from Sarabande Books and was published in 2001. Her second book, *Fragment of the Head of a Queen*, appeared from Sarabande in 2007. Her third book, *Oracle*, was published by Norton in 2015. A professor of English and creative writing at the City University of New York's College of Staten Island, she is the recipient of a Kate Tufts Discovery Prize, a Whiting Award, and a Guggenheim Fellowship. She lives in southern Maine.

Poetry is vital to language and living. Since 1972, Copper Canyon Press has published extraordinary poetry from around the world to engage the imaginations and intellects of readers, writers, booksellers, librarians, teachers, students, and donors.

COPPER CANYON PRESS WISHES TO EXTEND A SPECIAL THANKS
TO THE FOLLOWING SUPPORTERS WHO PROVIDED FUNDING
DURING THE COVID-19 PANDEMIC:

4Culture
Academy of American Poets (Literary Relief Fund)
City of Seattle Office of Arts & Culture
Community of Literary Magazines and Presses (Literary Relief Fund)
Economic Development Council of Jefferson County
National Book Foundation (Literary Relief Fund)
Poetry Foundation
U.S. Department of the Treasury Payroll Protection Program

WE ARE GRATEFUL FOR THE MAJOR SUPPORT

PROVIDED BY:

THE PAUL G. ALLEN
FAMILY FOUNDATION

WE ARE GRATEFUL FOR THE MAJOR SUPPORT
PROVIDED BY:

The Chinese character for poetry is made up of two parts:
"word" and "temple." It also serves as pressmark for
Copper Canyon Press.

The poems are set in Adobe Caslon Pro.
Book design and composition by Phil Kovacevich.